# REFLECTIONS
FOR
**LENT** 2025

# REFLECTIONS
## FOR
# LENT

Wednesday 5 March –
Saturday 19 April 2025

JUSTINE ALLAIN CHAPMAN
MALCOLM GUITE
JOHN PERUMBALATH

with Holy Week reflections by
DAVID FORD

Church House Publishing
Church House
Great Smith Street
London SW1P 3AZ

ISBN 978 1 78140 484 3

Published 2024 by Church House Publishing
Copyright © The Archbishops' Council 2024

The opinions expressed in this book are those of the authors and do not necessarily reflect the official policy of the General Synod or The Archbishops' Council of the Church of England.

Series editor: Catherine Williams
Liturgical editor: Peter Moger
Designed and typeset by Hugh Hillyard-Parker
Printed and bound by CPI Group (UK) Ltd, Croydon, CR0 4YY

What do you think of *Reflections for Lent*?

We'd love to hear from you – simply email us at

**publishing@churchofengland.org**

or write to us at

Church House Publishing, Church House,
Great Smith Street, London SW1P 3AZ.

Visit **www.dailyprayer.org.uk** for more information on the *Reflections* series, ordering and subscriptions.

# Contents

# About the authors

**Justine Allain Chapman** served as a parish priest and in theological education specializing in mission and pastoral care. She is currently Archdeacon of Boston in the Diocese of Lincoln committed to the wellbeing of clergy, congregations and churches. Her most recent book, *The Resilient Disciple*, is for Lent.

**Stephen Cottrell** is the Archbishop of York, having previously been Bishop of Chelmsford. He is a well-known writer and speaker on evangelism, spirituality and catechesis. He is one of the team that produced *Pilgrim*, the popular course for the Christian Journey.

**David F. Ford OBE** is Regius Professor of Divinity Emeritus in the University of Cambridge, a Fellow of Selwyn College and a Reader in the Church of England. He is co-chair of the Rose Castle Foundation and the author of *The Gospel of John. A Theological Commentary* and (with Ashley Cocksworth) of *Glorification and the Life of Faith*.

**Malcolm Guite** is a life fellow of Girton College, Cambridge, a poet and author of *What do Christians Believe?; Faith, Hope and Poetry; Sounding the Seasons: One hundred and ten sonnets for the Christian Year; The Singing Bowl; Word in the Wilderness; Mariner: A voyage with Samuel Taylor Coleridge*, and *David's Crown: Sounding the Psalms*. He also writes the 'Poet's Corner' column for *The Church Times*.

**Mark Oakley** is Dean of Southwark. Prior to this he was Dean and Fellow of St John's College, Cambridge. He is also Honorary Canon Theologian of Wakefield Cathedral in the Diocese of Leeds. He is the author of *The Collage of God* (2001), *The Splash of Words: Believing in Poetry* (2016) and *My Sour Sweet Days: George Herbert and the Journey of the Soul* (2019) as well as numerous articles and reviews, usually in the areas of faith, poetry, human rights and literature. He is a Fellow of King's College London, where he is also a Visiting Lecturer.

**John Perumbalath** is the Bishop of Liverpool, having previously been Archdeacon of Barking and Bishop of Bradwell. He has served as a theological educator and parish priest in the dioceses of Calcutta (Church of North India) and Rochester. He regularly guest lectures in the fields of faith and social engagement and in biblical studies.

**Rachel Treweek** is Bishop of Gloucester and the first female diocesan bishop in England. She served in two parishes in London and was Archdeacon of Northolt and later Hackney. Prior to ordination she was a speech and language therapist and is a trained practitioner in conflict transformation.

## About *Reflections for Lent*

Based on the *Common Worship Lectionary* readings for Morning Prayer, these daily reflections are designed to refresh and inspire times of personal prayer. The aim is to provide rich, contemporary and engaging insights into Scripture.

Each page lists the lectionary readings for the day, with the main psalms for that day highlighted in **bold**. The collect of the day – either the *Common Worship* collect or the shorter additional collect – is also included.

For those using this book in conjunction with a service of Morning Prayer, the following conventions apply: a psalm printed in parentheses is omitted if it has been used as the opening canticle at that office; a psalm marked with an asterisk may be shortened if desired.

A short reflection is provided on either the Old or New Testament reading. Popular writers, experienced ministers, biblical scholars and theologians contribute to this series, all bringing their own emphases, enthusiasms and approaches to biblical interpretation.

Regular users of Morning Prayer and *Time to Pray* (from *Common Worship: Daily Prayer*) and anyone who follows the Lectionary for their regular Bible reading will benefit from the rich variety of traditions represented in these stimulating and accessible pieces.

The book also includes both a simple form of Common Worship: Morning Prayer (see pages 48–49) and a short form of Night Prayer, also known as Compline (see pages 52–55), particularly for the benefit of those readers who are new to the habit of the Daily Office or for any reader while travelling.

## Lent – jousting within the self

It has been said that the heart of the human problem is the problem of the human heart. Lent is time set aside each year to take this thought seriously.

A few years ago, there was a story in the papers about a painting by Pieter Bruegel the Elder. It is currently on display in Vienna's marvellous Kunsthistorisches Museum, but Krakow's National Museum claims it is theirs and that it was stolen by the wife of the city's Nazi governor in 1939 during the occupation of Poland.

The painting is called 'The Fight Between Carnival and Lent' and it was painted in 1559. It is a beautifully typical Bruegel painting. It is a large, crowded canvas with nearly 200 men, women and children depicted on it. We find ourselves looking down on a town square during a riotous festival. The painting can be looked at in two halves. On the right, we see a church with people leaving after prayer. We see them giving alms to the poor, feeding the hungry, helping those with disability, calling attention to their need and tending to the dying. On the left, we see an inn. Congregated around it are beer drinkers, gamblers, various saucy types. The vulnerable nearby are not noticed, including a solitary procession of lepers. Instead, a man vomits out of a window and another bangs his head against a wall.

In the foreground, we see two figures being pulled towards each other on floats. One is Lady Lent, gaunt and unshowy, dressed as a nun, with followers eating pretzels and fish as well as drawing fresh water from a large well. The other is Carnival, a fat figure, armed with a meat spit and a pork pie helmet. He's followed by masked carousers. A man in yellow – the symbolic colour of deceit – pushes his float, though he looks rather weighed down by cups and a bag of belongings. In the background, we see, on the left, some stark, leafless trees, but on the right side, buds are awakening on the branches and, as if to see them better, a woman is busily cleaning her windows.

It is an allegorical delight, and we might do worse than take a close look at it sometime this Lent. It's tempting to classify each human there as either good or bad, secular or faithful, kind or indifferent. We love to place people into convenient cutlery trays, dividing us all up as is most useful for us. What I love about this painting, however, is that it reminds me that we are all similarly made with two halves.

For so many of us, there is a constant fight going on within between the times we are negligent and the times we are careful; days in which we get through with a self that enjoys its own attention, being centre-stage, and days when our self just feels somehow more itself when not being selfish. I have an impulse to pray; I have an impulse to avoid or forget it. There are parts of me grotesquely masked, and there are parts of me trying to clean my windows on a ladder, as it were, wanting to increase transparency and attention to the world, to me and to my relationships.

Lent begins with a small dusty cross being made on my head, the hard case that protects the organ that makes decisions. The season starts by asking me to imagine how life might be if the imprint of Christ's courageous compassion might make itself felt and acted on, rather than just passionately talked about. Lent knows what we are like. It has seen the painting. It has read a bit of Freud, some history books, political manifestos and memoirs of hurt and achievement. It winces at our cyclical, self-destructive repetitions. It believes in us, though, knowing that, with God and each other, if we reach outside of our own hardened little worlds, we set the scene to be helped and, maybe, even changed. That would be good – for me and those who live with me.

In the Gospels, the 40 days Jesus spent in the beguiling wilderness immediately followed his baptism. Coming up out of the water, he had heard the unmistakable voice that matters, telling him he was cherished, wanted and ready. He then goes into the heat spending time with himself, hearing other voices that want him to live down to them; but he knows that his vocation can only be lived when he learns to live up to the one voice he heard that day in the river, not down to the ones that want him to live some conventionally indifferent and submerged existence as a consumer of the world and not as a citizen of the kingdom. We follow him. Where he goes, so do we. A wilderness Lent is needed more than ever to do some heart-repair and start becoming Christians again.

I don't know who owns the Bruegel painting. What I do know is that its themes belong to all of us; our inner landscape matches his rowdy town square. As long as the fight continues, the soul will be alive.

*Mark Oakley*

3

## Building daily prayer into daily life

In our morning routines there are many tasks we do without giving much thought to them, and others that we do with careful attention. Daily prayer and Bible reading is a strange mixture of these. These are disciplines (and gifts) that we as Christians should have in our daily pattern, but they are not tasks to be ticked off. Rather they are a key component of our developing relationship with God. In them is *life* – for the fruits of this time are to be lived out by us – and to be most fruitful, the task requires both purpose and letting go.

In saying a daily office of prayer, we make a deliberate decision to spend time with God – the God who is always with us. In prayer and attentive reading of the Scriptures, there is both a conscious entering into God's presence and a 'letting go' of all we strive to control: both are our acknowledgement that it is God who is God.

*… come before his presence with a song…*

*Know that the Lord is God;*
*it is he that has made us and we are his;*
*we are his people and the sheep of his pasture.*

*Enter his gates with thanksgiving…*

> *(Psalm 100, a traditional Canticle at Morning Prayer)*

If we want a relationship with someone to deepen and grow, we need to spend time with that person. It can be no surprise that the same is true between us and God.

In our daily routines, I suspect that most of us intentionally look in the mirror; occasionally we might see beyond the surface of our external reflection and catch a glimpse of who we truly are. For me, a regular pattern of daily prayer and Bible reading is like a hard look in a clean mirror: it gives a clear reflection of myself, my life and the world in which I live. But it is more than that, for in it I can also see the reflection of God who is most clearly revealed in Jesus Christ and present with us now in the Holy Spirit.

This commitment to daily prayer is about our relationship with the God who is love. St Paul, in his great passage about love, speaks of now seeing 'in a mirror, dimly' but one day seeing face to face: 'Now I know only in part; then I will know fully, even as I have been fully known' (1 Corinthians 13.12). Our daily prayer is part of that seeing in a mirror dimly, and it is also part of our deep yearning for an ever-clearer vision of our God. As we read Scripture, the past and the future converge in the present moment. We hear words from long ago – some of which can appear strange and confusing – and yet, the Holy Spirit is living and active in the present. In this place of relationship and revelation, we open ourselves to the possibility of being changed, of being reshaped in a way that is good for us and all creation.

It is important that the words of prayer and scripture should penetrate deep within rather than be a mere veneer. A quiet location is therefore a helpful starting point. For some, domestic circumstances or daily schedule make that difficult, but it is never impossible to become more fully present to God. The depths of our being can still be accessed no matter the world's clamour and activity. An awareness of this is all part of our journey from a false sense of control to a place of letting go, to a place where there is an opportunity for transformation.

Sometimes in our attention to Scripture there will be connection with places of joy or pain; we might be encouraged or provoked or both. As we look and see and encounter God more deeply, there will be thanksgiving and repentance; the cries of our heart will surface as we acknowledge our needs and desires for ourselves and the world. The liturgy of Morning Prayer gives this voice and space.

I find it helpful to begin Morning Prayer by lighting a candle. This marks my sense of purpose and my acknowledgement of Christ's presence with me. It is also a silent prayer for illumination as I prepare to be attentive to what I see in the mirror, both of myself and of God. Amid the revelation of Scripture and the cries of my heart, the constancy of the tiny flame bears witness to the hope and light of Christ in all that is and will be.

When the candle is extinguished, I try to be still as I watch the smoke disappear. For me, it is symbolic of my prayers merging with the day. I know that my prayer and the reading of Scripture are not the smoke and mirrors of delusion. Rather, they are about encounter and discovery as I seek to venture into the day to love and serve the Lord as a disciple of Jesus Christ.

+ *Rachel Treweek*

## Lectio Divina – a way of reading the Bible

*Lectio Divina* is a contemplative way of reading the Bible. It dates back to the early centuries of the Christian Church and was established as a monastic practice by Benedict in the sixth century. It is a way of praying the Scriptures that leads us deeper into God's word. We slow down. We read a short passage more than once. We chew it over slowly and carefully. We savour it. Scripture begins to speak to us in a new way. It speaks to us personally, and aids that union we have with God through Christ, who is himself the Living Word.

Make sure you are sitting comfortably. Breathe slowly and deeply. Ask God to speak to you through the passage that you are about to read.

This way of praying starts with our silence. We often make the mistake of thinking prayer is about what we say to God. It is actually the other way round. God wants to speak to us. He will do this through the Scriptures. So don't worry about what to say. Don't worry if nothing jumps out at you at first. God is patient. He will wait for the opportunity to get in. He will give you a word and lead you to understand its meaning for you today.

### First reading: Listen

As you read the passage listen for a word or phrase that attracts you. Allow it to arise from the passage as if it is God's word for you today. Sit in silence repeating the word or phrase in your head.

Then say the word or phrase aloud.

### Second reading: Ponder

As you read the passage again, ask how this word or phrase speaks to your life and why it has connected with you. Ponder it carefully. Don't worry if you get distracted – it may be part of your response to offer to God. Sit in silence and then frame a single sentence that begins to say aloud what this word or phrase says to you.

### Third reading: Pray

As you read the passage for the last time, ask what Christ is calling from you. What is it that you need to do or consider or relinquish or take on as a result of what God is saying to you in this word or phrase? In the silence that follows the reading, pray for the grace of the Spirit to plant this word in your heart.

If you are in a group, talk for a few minutes and pray with each other.

If you are on your own, speak your prayer to God either aloud or in the silence of your heart.

If there is time, you may even want to read the passage a fourth time, and then end with the same silence before God with which you began.

*++Stephen Cottrell*

## **Wednesday 5 March**

Ash Wednesday

Psalm **38**
Daniel 9.3-6, 17-19
1 Timothy 6.6-19

### **1 Timothy 6.6-19**

*'… there is great gain in godliness with contentment' (v.6)*

Keeping a holy Lent involves paying attention to how we live. How we regard and use money are among the most important ways in which Christian understanding challenges and transforms sinful cultural norms. These attitudes and practices are part of making a 'good confession', which is a commandment for believers, not an optional extra in Christian life.

If we are to have a proper Christian attitude, it is necessary to understand 'gain' and 'profit' beyond material terms. The author writes of death in verse 7. The dead have no use for money, but their godliness and personal integrity (the word translated as contentment could mean integrity too) are spoken of as 'great gain' beyond the grave.

The instruction of what to avoid and what to pursue comes from the ethical discourses of antiquity: it portrays what kind of character is expected of the people of God. We cannot simply flee away from the love of money, or from the vices referred to in verse 4, without consciously embracing a spiritual disposition and moral character. This is expanded in terms of six virtues – righteousness, godliness, faith, love, endurance and gentleness.

Formation of this spiritual and moral character is traditionally a focus of Lent. This will lead us to do good, to be generous and rich in good works. This passage offers us so much material for reflection on the usual Lenten themes of piety, detachment and giving.

COLLECT

Almighty and everlasting God,
you hate nothing that you have made
and forgive the sins of all those who are penitent:
create and make in us new and contrite hearts
that we, worthily lamenting our sins
and acknowledging our wretchedness,
may receive from you, the God of all mercy,
perfect remission and forgiveness;
through Jesus Christ our Lord.

8 | *Reflection by* **John Perumbalath**

Psalm **77** *or* 90, **92**
Jeremiah 2.14-32
John 4.1-26

# Thursday 6 March

### John 4.1-26

*'Jesus said to her, "Give me a drink".' (v.7)*

Jesus' action here is in serious violation of the prevailing cultural code. It transcended all the barriers of gender, race and religion that existed at that time. There were clear boundaries between 'chosen people' and 'rejected people', and between male and female. Also, that this woman came to fetch water at noon rather than joining the social occasion in the morning or evening suggests that she was already an outsider in her own community.

Jesus disregards the woman's protest of the impropriety of the situation and brings up her past and the present not to shame her, but to take away their power in showing how little they affect how God accepts her. What Jesus offers her is a role reversal: instead of her being the one who gives water, she could become the one who receives. And Jesus names obvious and hidden thirsts to deepen the woman's awareness of both.

By tendering direct questions and diverting her distracting responses by more intimate questions, both gain a deeper knowledge of the other and realize that water in the well is not the endpoint of this conversation, but just its beginning. Bodily needs for basic sustenance and a spiritual tapestry of relationship are woven into this encounter that leads to further questioning, the healthy airing of confusion, impassioned testimony, defensive disbelief, and confession of faith. The story shows us how effective faith conversations might take place and how God meets us where we are and receives us.

Holy God,
our lives are laid open before you:
rescue us from the chaos of sin
and through the death of your Son
bring us healing and make us whole
in Jesus Christ our Lord.

COLLECT

*Reflection by* **John Perumbalath**      9

# Friday 7 March

Psalms **3**, 7 *or* **88** (95)
Jeremiah 3.6-22
John 4.27-42

### John 4.27-42

*'He cannot be the Messiah, can he?' (v.29)*

The woman has now moved from protest and doubt to confession and witness. The content of her witness seems tentative, in the form of a question rather than a convincing statement, but it's enough to lead her villagers to Jesus. Bearing compelling witness does not depend on our absolute certainty in everything we say but on our honest willingness to share what we have experienced with an invitation to 'come and see'.

Jesus' disciples do not seem to be in a different place than that of the Samaritan woman when they come back with food. The misunderstanding, wordplay, and double meaning that we found in the previous conversations are here too in the conversation between Jesus and his disciples about food and harvest. Despite being close followers of Jesus, they still lacked understanding.

Jesus speaks with the disciples about his vocation and the vocation of all his witnesses, setting out some general principles. They are to feed on a different food: the food of doing the will of God. They do not need to wait for a future harvest: the fields are always ripe for God's witnesses. And, finally, they are not to do all the work. We build on the labour of others and leave space for others to continue after us.

COLLECT

Almighty and everlasting God,
you hate nothing that you have made
and forgive the sins of all those who are penitent:
create and make in us new and contrite hearts
that we, worthily lamenting our sins
and acknowledging our wretchedness,
may receive from you, the God of all mercy,
perfect remission and forgiveness;
through Jesus Christ our Lord.

*Reflection by* **John Perumbalath**

Psalm **71** *or* 96, **97**, 100
Jeremiah 4.1-18
John 4.43-end

### John 4.43-end

*'Go; your son will live' (v.50)*

The first sign in Cana of water changed into wine had revealed Jesus' glory. Here, in the second, he is revealed as life-giver. The royal official moves from a request for help, through astonished realization of Jesus' power, to a firm commitment to Jesus. He approached Jesus for healing of his son, but he also receives the gift of faith. Jesus now draws to himself a family identified with royal court, in addition to the Jewish disciples and Samaritans he has already gathered, building his diverse beloved community.

Faith based on a sign is not enough, but it can be a stage on the way to a relationship with the one to which the sign points. It is the presence of God that transforms Jesus' acts from miracles to signs. Signs hold together the spiritual and physical in the same way as they are held together in the life of Jesus, the Word incarnate. It is not the miracle itself, but the presence of God at work within the miracle that leads to faith.

Yet here it is physical healing that provides a glimpse of God's character in Jesus. God knows that we human beings experience the spiritual only through our physicality, and we need to remember this as we witness to Christ today. It was both physical and material realities that would become 'signs' of God's presence and glory.

Holy God,
our lives are laid open before you:
rescue us from the chaos of sin
and through the death of your Son
bring us healing and make us whole
in Jesus Christ our Lord.

COLLECT

*Reflection by* **John Perumbalath**     11

**Monday 10 March**

### John 5.1-18

*'Stand up, take your mat and walk' (v.8)*

The sick man here represents those who have given up on healing, fallen into apathy and in their hopelessness, tend to rely on pity. Jesus refuses to play the self-pity game, ignores the question of who is to blame, and tells the man to get up and walk. He rises and steps out in faith. Faith brings healing of a limitation, restoration of purpose and hope, and the prospects of a fruitful life. And the healing is more than physical: the restoration that Jesus offers is holistic: 'Do not sin anymore, so that nothing worse happens to you.'

Jesus' compassion takes the paralytic seriously. 'Do you want to be made well?' is a question that respects the dignity and freedom of the sick person. Encouraging a desire to be made well is a compassionate act towards someone who has, to all intents and purposes, given up hope.

The episode also speaks about the cost of ministry and the price we might have to pay in the ministry of liberation. We do not know whether the healed man was collaborating with Jesus' enemies, or it was simply a case of innocent answers to their probing questions. In any case, the healing provokes a negative reaction among them. For his enemies, Jesus was breaking the Sabbath rules, but Jesus affirmed that God worked on the Sabbath. We cannot restrain God's work through the regulations and traditions we establish for ourselves.

COLLECT

Almighty God,
whose Son Jesus Christ fasted forty days in the wilderness,
and was tempted as we are, yet without sin:
give us grace to discipline ourselves in obedience to your Spirit;
and, as you know our weakness,
so may we know your power to save;
through Jesus Christ our Lord.

*Reflection by* **John Perumbalath**

Psalm **44** *or* **106**\* (*or* 103)  **Tuesday 11 March**
Jeremiah 5.1-19
John 5.19-29

### John 5.19-29

*'... those who hear will live' (v.25)*

Having identified himself with the Father in the previous episode, Jesus goes on to talk in depth about the dynamic divine unity in today's reading. He makes a distinction between himself and God but without any functional difference: 'whatever the Father does, the Son does likewise.' The relationship between the Father and the Son cannot be reduced to a rational formula; rather it points to the mystery of God's nature.

Some scholars simplify the fourth evangelist's teaching about the future as realized: John teaches that God's future is already come in Jesus Christ. Verses 26-27 are clear in speaking about the here and now. But John's theology is not devoid of future hope. Verses 27-29 presuppose a future resurrection and judgement. Like John, we need to hold this tension between present and future: the Christ has come but the Christ is still to come.

The discourse also lays out the expected outcome of God's work through his Son. People need to 'hear'. Hearing is not only listening to the words but also receiving and accepting the message. This enables them to 'live' or have eternal life, a life that begins with God now. And those who have this life from Christ will be doers of good. Accepting God, enjoying eternal life and doing good are essential ingredients of the life expected of us.

Heavenly Father,
your Son battled with the powers of darkness,
and grew closer to you in the desert:
help us to use these days to grow in wisdom and prayer
that we may witness to your saving love
in Jesus Christ our Lord.

COLLECT

*Reflection by* **John Perumbalath**    13

## Wednesday 12 March

Psalms **6**, 17 *or* 110, **111**, 112
Jeremiah 5.20-end
John 5.30-end

### John 5.30-end

*'There is another who testifies on my behalf ... ' (v.32)*

Jesus affirms that God alone is an adequate witness: that the Father who sent him has testified on his behalf. God does not witness directly but through a variety of mediators. Jesus lists some of these, helping us to know where we can find God's witness. Jewish law required two or three witnesses in serious allegations (e.g. Deuteronomy 17.6; Numbers 35.30) and in his ongoing debate with the Jews, Jesus here summons witnesses to support his case.

God uses human agency. The first witness Jesus calls for is John the Baptist, the one who came to prepare his way. The Evangelist has already established the Baptist's testimony earlier in the Gospel. Jesus then speaks about a testimony greater than John's – the works of God that Jesus does. Jesus' enemies often had a problem with Jesus' works. They sometimes found it difficult to reject his works as being from the devil because of the popularity he was gaining. Equally, they could not reject these works in God's name because they would then be seen as having rejected God.

Finally, Jesus moves on to the witness that his critics cannot avoid – the scriptures. His critics claimed their beliefs and practices were rooted in scripture: they often weaponized scripture to discredit him. They uphold scripture religiously and often literally, but they fail to read it with an openness to hear what God might be saying through it.

COLLECT

Almighty God,
whose Son Jesus Christ fasted forty days in the wilderness,
and was tempted as we are, yet without sin:
give us grace to discipline ourselves in obedience to your Spirit;
and, as you know our weakness,
so may we know your power to save;
through Jesus Christ our Lord.

| *Reflection by* **John Perumbalath**

Psalms **42**, 43 *or* 113, **115**　　　　　　**Thursday 13 March**
Jeremiah 6.9-21
John 6.1-15

### John 6.1-15
*'But what are they among so many people?' (v.9)*

The feeding of the five thousand is the only miracle story we find in all four Gospels. John uses it in a specific way that prepares us for Jesus' discourse on the bread of life. Jesus' action in taking, giving thanks and distributing the loaves will trigger thoughts of the eucharist for many readers. Jesus, meeting his hearers where they are, uses everyday substance from their daily lives and leads them to a life-changing choice.

But the occasion here where Jesus' glory is revealed is one of normal human need: hunger. There is no jumping straight into the spiritual need without dealing first with the immediate physical need. The miracle shows Jesus' concern for both This is a story that reveals God's compassionate love, and with the overtones of the Eucharist, it resonates strongly with Jesus' sacrificial self-giving in response to the human condition.

We need also to pay attention to the other characters in the story. Philip's answer expresses his despair at Jesus' question and reflects our general helplessness in the face of challenging situations of human need. Andrew jumps in with helpful information about the boy's lunch pack although he thought it inadequate. The boy, though, is willing to offer what he had, although very simple (barley was inferior to wheat). As Desmond Tutu said, 'The divine miracle requires the thoroughly inadequate human contribution.' God creates abundance from the very little that we can offer.

> Heavenly Father,
> your Son battled with the powers of darkness,
> and grew closer to you in the desert:
> help us to use these days to grow in wisdom and prayer
> that we may witness to your saving love
> in Jesus Christ our Lord.

COLLECT

*Reflection by* **John Perumbalath**　　│　15

## Friday 14 March

Psalm **22** *or* **139**
Jeremiah 6.22-end
John 6.16-27

### John 6.16-27

*'It is I; do not be afraid' (v.20)*

Today's reading describes the most dramatic self-revelation of Jesus to this point in John's Gospel. Jesus' demonstration of power over the sea followed by an 'I am' saying presents a claim to speak both for and as God. There is no confession of faith from the disciples as in Matthew's account of this story (14.33) nor confusion among them as in Mark's (6.51-52). This is more about what Jesus does, and less about the impact of his revelation.

Jesus walks across the sea and brings his disciples safely to their destination. This is so unlike what the crowd had expected when they sought to make him king. He is not presented here as a candidate for public position and power but rather as God's own presence coming to his disciples. Jesus moves away from the crowd that wants him to be king and instead reveals himself in the midst of the disciple's fears.

The crowd reappears (v.22) and, in response to or in search of Jesus' signs, goes to the other side of the lake to meet him. The crowd represents the struggle of those who are open to believing, but neither the scriptures nor the signs lead them to a deeper commitment. The evangelist is building his invitation to all his readers to move from simple openness to faith in the presence of a sign to a mature faith that will no longer depend on signs.

COLLECT

Almighty God,
whose Son Jesus Christ fasted forty days in the wilderness,
and was tempted as we are, yet without sin:
give us grace to discipline ourselves in obedience to your Spirit;
and, as you know our weakness,
so may we know your power to save;
through Jesus Christ our Lord.

*Reflection by* **John Perumbalath**

Psalms 59, **63** *or* 120, **121**, 122
Jeremiah 7.1-20
John 6.27-40

## Saturday 15 March

### John 6.27-40

*'Sir, give us this bread always' (v.34)*

The question 'What must we do to perform the works of God?' suggests that the crowd is beginning to accept Jesus' challenge to think beyond physical food and to consider the things of God. When they go looking for a sign again, Jesus brings them back to the concerns beyond material food by speaking about the bread from heaven.

The crowd seems to be suggesting that, despite their hunger, they don't really know what they want. Jesus then focuses the conversation, speaking not about 'works' – the good deeds that make up life – but about a single 'work': to believe in the one who has been sent. But this requirement of faith has challenging implications for discipleship: believing is not for self-satisfaction or gain.

We might read 'all that he has given me' as implying that there are others who are not given to him. But John's emphasis on 'believing' necessitates that we hold human and divine responsibility in tension. Both God and humans play a role in having faith. God gives us the bread from heaven, but we must seek and receive it, acknowledging our hunger and thirst that bread and water alone cannot fulfil (v.35). This bread is given by God in the person of Christ and we receive him in the 'work' of faith.

Heavenly Father,
your Son battled with the powers of darkness,
and grew closer to you in the desert:
help us to use these days to grow in wisdom and prayer
that we may witness to your saving love
in Jesus Christ our Lord.

COLLECT

## Monday 17 March

### John 6.41-51

*'I am the living bread' (v.51)*

It is still the case that whatever question you ask children in church or school worship someone is likely to give the answer 'Jesus'. After all, it has a fair chance of being right and may well satisfy the vicar at least in the short term. The crowd Jesus addresses also prefers to stick to the expected answers about where Jesus comes from: his parentage rather than his claim that he is the bread of life come down from heaven. Like their ancestors in the wilderness, who were content once they knew they could collect manna every day, they are looking for bread to satisfy them now rather than the bread of eternal life.

In this season of Lent, we recall Jesus' words in the wilderness, that human beings 'cannot live by bread alone'. We pray for God to give us 'our daily bread' in the Lord's Prayer and in doing so are grateful for both physical and spiritual sustenance, for manna for the day and the bread of life for eternity.

Then, as now, there are those who because of the loud voices of many religious people claiming that they are in the right cannot hear the life-giving words of Jesus. Today might we listen more deeply into situations and be open to answers beyond our expectations that only Jesus can bring?

COLLECT

Almighty God,
you show to those who are in error the light of your truth,
that they may return to the way of righteousness:
grant to all those who are admitted
    into the fellowship of Christ's religion,
that they may reject those things
    that are contrary to their profession,
and follow all such things as are agreeable to the same;
through our Lord Jesus Christ.

*Reflection by* **Justine Allain Chapman**

Psalm **50** *or* **132**, 133
Jeremiah 8.1-15
John 6.52-59

# Tuesday 18 March

### John 6.52-59

*'... whoever eats me will live because of me' (v.57)*

Several members of my family are coeliac. If they eat anything made with wheat or containing gluten they become ill. So now we look for bread made with some other kind of flour, and that goes for communion wafers too. Having to make changes to the basics of what we ate was irritating, disappointing and expensive, but change was necessary for us to eat together and provide healthy and nourishing meals.

Far beyond God providing manna or a household sharing food, Jesus describes himself as the bread of life; believers eating his human flesh and swilling it down with his human blood. It was a shocking and distasteful image then, and even though as Christians we can quickly shift from thoughts of cannibalism to the Eucharist, it is still vivid and uncomfortable.

Real participation in Christ and Christ's body goes beyond intellectual assent or good table manners. Communion with Christ is a sharing and abiding in the divine life force that transforms us. We participate in this communion individually and as one body, seeking a holiness and wholeness that attends not only to our minds and bodies, but also to our social and political relating. Our 'amen' when we receive the Sacrament at Holy Communion is our acceptance that we are ever becoming the body of Christ, together.

If you eat bread today, might you acknowledge Christ as the bread of life and pause to abide in him?

Almighty God,
by the prayer and discipline of Lent
may we enter into the mystery of Christ's sufferings,
and by following in his Way
come to share in his glory;
through Jesus Christ our Lord.

COLLECT

*Reflection by* **Justine Allain Chapman**  |  19

## **Wednesday 19 March**

Joseph of Nazareth

Psalms 25, 147.1-12
Isaiah 11.1-10
Matthew 13.54-end

### **Matthew 13.54-end**

*'Is not this the carpenter's son?' (v.55)*

'Tall poppy syndrome' is a term from Australia and New Zealand and it occurs when peers think you are getting above your station, too successful or boastful, and cut you down to size by criticism and exclusion. In Nazareth the people were astounded by Jesus' teaching, but bewildered and resentful that one of their own should have gained such wisdom and attention. Jesus identified this as what happens to prophets – they are without honour in the place where they come from. So, because of their unbelief, Jesus did not do many deeds of power.

Today we honour Joseph of Nazareth who was no tall poppy. His calling was hidden and humble as he protected both the reputation and life of the family given to him – he was a righteous man, unwilling to expose Mary to public disgrace (Matthew 1.19). If the people's unbelief prevented Jesus working deeds of power, Joseph's belief and care for his family enabled God's works of power to be revealed, for Jesus was shaped by the compassion, faith and practical wisdom he saw in Joseph. It was Joseph's belief in God's guidance through dreams and angels, putting his trust in God's working within Mary and giving Jesus his protection and an occupation, that gave shape to the divine life on earth.

Might we, as we remember Joseph, rather than cut someone down, show that we believe in them, knowing that such belief opens human life to the power of God?

COLLECT

God our Father,
who from the family of your servant David
raised up Joseph the carpenter
to be the guardian of your incarnate Son
and husband of the Blessed Virgin Mary:
give us grace to follow him
in faithful obedience to your commands;
through Jesus Christ our Lord.

*Reflection by* **Justine Allain Chapman**

Psalm **34** *or* **143**, 146
Jeremiah 9.12-24
John 7.1-13

**Thursday 20 March**

### John 7.1-13

*'... show yourself to the world' (v.4)*

It was hard every Sunday night to find something for our primary-school-aged children to 'Show and Tell' in school the next morning. We would affectionately call it 'Bring and Brag', not realizing then that later those same children would, along with us adults too, experience the pressures of social media requiring us to show something of our lives by a post and picture.

Jesus' brothers wanted to send him to Jerusalem to the festival so he and his works would be widely known, they said, but also so that they too could see how credible he was.

*Sukkot*, or the festivals of Booths, or Tabernacles, remembers the time of journeying through the wilderness. Households now as then make a temporary shelter, a *sukkah*, thankful for a more secure life as they celebrate God's protection and provision at that exposed and uncertain time where there was little to boast about.

In the forty days in the wilderness Jesus resisted the temptation to show off just as he did at this festival: conscious that his time is not yet at hand, he holds back.

In our culture of superficial news and constant scrutiny we, like Jesus, can be pushed to brag or to take up rather than give space. Today might we join Jesus in pondering that even when there are only temporary and insubstantial shelters to protect us, it is God in whom we find security?

Almighty God,
you show to those who are in error the light of your truth,
that they may return to the way of righteousness:
grant to all those who are admitted
into the fellowship of Christ's religion,
that they may reject those things
that are contrary to their profession,
and follow all such things as are agreeable to the same;
through our Lord Jesus Christ.

COLLECT

*Reflection by* **Justine Allain Chapman**

## Friday 21 March

### John 7.14-24

*'Do not judge by appearances' (v.24)*

As I gained experience as a school teacher, I shifted from teaching a subject, focusing on the content, to teaching the students. I became aware of how I could enable a year group, class or individual genuinely to learn, be inspired and make connections with other subjects and with their lives.

Jesus inspired astonishment in his hearers as he taught. Much of this was to do with the way in which his words rang true – how he met people's yearnings with life-giving words. His words, he says, are not his own nor for his glory, but will resonate deeply and be accepted as God's by anyone who seeks to do the will of God.

Jesus' hearers, proud of being law-abiding, circumcized on the sabbath, but condemned him for healing on the sabbath. Their judgement of him did not come from a place of openness to learning, change or growth.

Honing our judgements so that we look beyond appearances is what Jesus asks of his hearers. Rather than seeking to be persuaded of an opinion or being on the right side of an argument, might we cultivate openness to judging another's words by the good they bring about? Pray today that those decisions we have been a part of bear fruit, with the humility to change our mind if they do not.

COLLECT

Almighty God,
you show to those who are in error the light of your truth,
that they may return to the way of righteousness:
grant to all those who are admitted
    into the fellowship of Christ's religion,
that they may reject those things
    that are contrary to their profession,
and follow all such things as are agreeable to the same;
through our Lord Jesus Christ.

*Reflection by* **Justine Allain Chapman**

Psalms 3, **25** *or* 147
Jeremiah 10.17-24
John 7.25-36

# Saturday 22 March

### John 7.25-36

*'... his hour had not yet come' (v.30)*

In the popular science fiction television series *Doctor Who*, the Doctor is a Time Lord, one of an ancient race from the planet Gallifrey. Taking various human forms over time, the Doctor saves worlds from catastrophes by preventing the timeline from being subverted, because in the Tardis, they can travel through time. The Doctor does not always arrive with much time to spare, but being present to intervene at a key moment is the nature of the mission.

Jesus, present from the beginning of time (John 1.1), avoids being arrested several times because his 'hour has not yet come'. His movements are hard to track. He speaks of staying a little longer but then going where no one else can go. Living within time, Jesus is conscious of events gaining pace and coming together, of disciples he must prepare, of teaching he wants to convey, and the anticipation of suffering and death.

Approaching the third Sunday of Lent we see time marching on. Greek has two words for time: *chronos* is time that can be measured; *kairos* moments are those that change the nature of things, such as a pregnant woman knowing that it is time for her baby to come. These different experiences of time are always present in our lives. I am increasingly aware of the subtleties and mystery of the way God works in the world, how openness to God through prayer enables encounters in time to shimmer with grace from above. Be open to notice this action of God today.

Almighty God,
by the prayer and discipline of Lent
may we enter into the mystery of Christ's sufferings,
and by following in his Way
come to share in his glory;
through Jesus Christ our Lord.

COLLECT

*Reflection by* **Justine Allain Chapman**    23

## Monday 24 March

### John 7.37-52

*'Out of a believer's heart shall flow' (v.38)*

In positive psychology the concept of flow describes the experience of being fully immersed in a feeling of energized focus. It is not overwhelming or understimulating but a joyful melting of action and consciousness. We might describe the things that absorb us, such as climbing or painting, where we experience 'being in the zone' or the flow state.

At the festival of Sukkot, the crowd sees the golden pitcher of water brought from the Pool of Siloam to the Temple and hears Jesus using the image of water to call the thirsty to him. He promises that believers who drink of him will experience his life flowing through them, as a river, steady and continuous, bringing life to all that surrounds it. It is such a contrast to the conflictual discussions among the crowd, the Temple police and the religious leaders – none of whom can decide whether Jesus' words are astounding or deceptive, his origins of God or of Galilee.

Nicodemus tried to stem the antagonism to Jesus by suggesting he is given a fair hearing. He already knew that Jesus requires something more than mental assent, that we must be born from above (John 3.3). Then, as now, Jesus calls us to change from within. As you pray, invite Jesus to transform you from within, sweeping away whatever may stem the flow of his life within your heart.

| | |
|---|---|
| **C O L L E C T** | Almighty God, |
| | whose most dear Son went not up to joy |
| | but first he suffered pain, |
| | and entered not into glory before he was crucified: |
| | mercifully grant that we, walking in the way of the cross, |
| | may find it none other than the way of life and peace; |
| | through Jesus Christ our Lord. |

| *Reflection by* **Justine Allain Chapman**

Psalms 111, 113
1 Samuel 2.1-10
Romans 5.12-end

# Tuesday 25 March

## Annunciation of Our Lord
## to the Blessed Virgin Mary

### Romans 5.12-end

*'... the free gift is not like the trespass' (v.15)*

Paul's discussion of trespass and law could be symbolized by a quill made of a single feather. He dips the tip into ink again and again to make sense of the dynamics of salvation, of the work God brought about through Christ. He contrasts Adam and Christ, sin and grace, obedience and disobedience and, implicitly, Eve and Mary.

On this day when we celebrate the angel Gabriel announcing to Mary that she will bear Jesus, it is a symbol of the angel's wings, swift and vast, feathers soft and strong, which reveals the contrast between sin and grace – that the free gift is not like the trespass. Only the unmerited gift of grace can undo the dominance of death and bring about the promise of life, eternal in its scope.

Mary's welcome of the angel's words that she was the 'favoured one' (Luke 1.28) begins the most profound upward spiral of grace in the life of humanity. Whereas sin separates us from God, the angel's words lead Mary to bear God's Son living a life of grace where God is at work. The method is not transactional but relational, and by the incarnation the opposites of human and divine, heaven and earth, come together as one. Dualism gives way to all things being held together in Christ (Colossians 1.17).

Today, might you notice where a vicious cycle could, by the flutter of an angel's wing, become a spiral of grace?

We beseech you, O Lord,
pour your grace into our hearts,
that as we have known the incarnation of your Son Jesus Christ
by the message of an angel,
so by his cross and passion
we may be brought to the glory of his resurrection;
through Jesus Christ our Lord.

COLLECT

## Wednesday 26 March

### John 8.12-30

*'Whoever follows ... will have the light of life' (v.12)*

The origin of the word 'Lent' comes from 'lengthening' because the days, in the northern hemisphere, are getting longer with less darkness and more light. Light and darkness are themes that run through John's Gospel with their double meanings of natural sight, daylight and insight or enlightenment.

As Lent progresses, although there are more hours of daylight, the darkness of human minds, proud and afraid, closes in around Jesus and threatens his life. Jesus declares himself to the 'light of the world' and that his followers need never walk in darkness because they have the light of life.

The experience of suffering, our own or another's, can feel like the descent of darkness immobilizing us. As with a beam of light from a torch showing us the next step, but little more, what really matters often becomes clear; we are able to walk forward because we experience love and fellowship, compassion and care. It is afterwards, when we look back on those times, that we might gain insight.

In the darkness of our world today in what form do we see the light that is Christ? If there seems to be more darkness than light, perhaps pray in these words written by a Jewish prisoner on the wall of the Nazi concentration camp: 'I believe in the sun, even when it is not shining. I believe in love, even when there's no one there. I believe in God, even when he is silent.'

COLLECT

Almighty God,
whose most dear Son went not up to joy
    but first he suffered pain,
and entered not into glory before he was crucified:
mercifully grant that we, walking in the way of the cross,
may find it none other than the way of life and peace;
through Jesus Christ our Lord.

| *Reflection by* **Justine Allain Chapman**

Psalms **56**, 57 *or* 14, **15**, 16
Jeremiah 14
John 8.31-47

# Thursday 27 March

### John 8.31-47

*'... you choose to do your father's desires' (v.44)*

Many people who have obtained their DNA profile have perhaps done so in order to deepen their sense of identity, or to gain some understanding of the strengths and vulnerabilities of their character. It's not for the fainthearted because you don't know what will be revealed. It can be deeply unsettling to discover a propensity for a life-limiting illness, or to learn that you are not actually biologically related to your grandfather. Our DNA profiles can tell us something about the way in which we have been shaped, but not who we are or how to respond to new knowledge about ourselves.

Jesus challenged the sense of entitlement his Jewish hearers felt in being descended from Abraham. He declared that for his disciples the truth about who he was and what they could become would set them free. But his proud hearers could not accept that they were not free. Seemingly having forgotten about being slaves in Egypt and seeking to kill Jesus they were, he said, the children of the devil who is the father of lies and a murderer. True descendants of Abraham would show his example of faith and character.

In Christ we have an identity where we are born anew and given power to become children of God (John 1.13). The legacy of the truth about anything in our past or background can be redeemed in Christ. Is there anyone that God calls you today to set free?

Eternal God,
give us insight
to discern your will for us,
to give up what harms us,
and to seek the perfection we are promised
in Jesus Christ our Lord.

COLLECT

*Reflection by* **Justine Allain Chapman**     27

**Friday 28 March**

Psalm **22** *or* 17, **19**
Jeremiah 15.10-end
John 8.48-end

### John 8.48-end

*'... whoever keeps my word will never see death' (v.51)*

Earlier in chapter 8 we read of Jesus' response to the scribes and Pharisees, and to the woman brought by them accused of adultery (8.1-11). She might well have been stoned, had Jesus not held up a mirror reflecting her persecutors' sin back to them.

The crowd in the Temple were by now unreceptive to Jesus and especially to the notion that they were not children of Abraham. Jesus experiences the violence of a crowd ready again with their stones, but this time they are for him. The woman was silenced by her experience. We know that Jesus will remain silent in the face of the final accusations against him, but before then, the crowd's insults and tone are menacing and the capacity to hear him further diminished.

By his dealings with people and by his teaching, Jesus tried to enable his hearers experience life with God as eternal and present in the here and now. Their argumentative response is a long way from such a spiritual path.

We should not be surprised that there are times when our Christian understanding of what it is to be human compels us to think and act differently from others around us. Nor that there are times when we cannot speak but must remain silent, withdrawing to reflect and pray. What will be the tone of our engagement with others today?

COLLECT

Almighty God,
whose most dear Son went not up to joy
    but first he suffered pain,
and entered not into glory before he was crucified:
mercifully grant that we, walking in the way of the cross,
may find it none other than the way of life and peace;
through Jesus Christ our Lord.

| *Reflection by* **Justine Allain Chapman**

## Saturday 29 March

### John 9.1-17

*'... who sinned, this man or his parents?' (v.2)*

It is natural for human beings to look for reasons for and causes of the way things are. It expands our knowledge, but it doesn't necessarily lead to any real insight or transformation. Bessel van der Kolk in the bestseller *The Body Keeps the Score: Mind, brain and body in the transformation of trauma*, identified the devastating effects of psychological trauma on the mind and body's development. Rather than focus on the causes, he movingly describes innovative treatments that can reactivate the brain's natural neuroplasticity and the tremendous power of our relationships to heal our minds and our bodies, opening the way to a new life post-trauma.

In a culture of blame, Jesus' disciples ask about causes – whether it was the parents' sin or the sin of the blind man himself that caused the blindness. Later, the crowd and the Pharisees want to know the reasons for the blind man's recovery of sight. Jesus is judged as a sinner, not one who has healing power from God, because he has healed on the sabbath. In both cases, the question about who should be judged a sinner motivates the questions about causes.

Judgementalism does not lead to healing and transformation. Today, notice the tendencies of your natural curiosity and pray that God may direct them towards insight and healing.

COLLECT

> Eternal God,
> give us insight
> to discern your will for us,
> to give up what harms us,
> and to seek the perfection we are promised
> in Jesus Christ our Lord.

## Monday 31 March

### John 9.18-end

*'Surely we are not blind, are we?' (v.40)*

Today's passage concludes the meditation on blindness and sight that began in chapter 8. It opens with a classic example of how people with disabilities are patronized by those who assume they can't speak for themselves, epitomized in the phrase 'Does he take sugar?' The religious authorities question the man's parents, assuming they will somehow know more than he does! His parents quite rightly reply, 'Ask him...he will speak for himself.'

And he certainly does. He dismantles the arguments of the 'authorities', and ends up wryly asking them if they too want to be Jesus' disciples, and they, like so many entitled people when they lose an argument, just revert to insult and exclusion: 'They drove him out.'

And then comes the real encounter with Jesus, and it's noteworthy that Jesus sought the man out, not the other way round. In the conversation that ensues Christ opens the man's eyes a second time, but this time he is granted spiritual sight and insight, and he recognizes Christ as Messiah, and worships him. And at precisely this moment of insight Jesus speaks his judgement against those who make themselves wilfully blind. Of course, we'd like to identify with the man born blind, transformed by Jesus, surely *we* are not blind, are we? But this story won't let us go so easily. We lift our eyes from the page wondering what our own wilful blindness might be concealing from us.

COLLECT

Merciful Lord,
absolve your people from their offences,
that through your bountiful goodness
we may all be delivered from the chains of those sins
which by our frailty we have committed;
grant this, heavenly Father,
for Jesus Christ's sake, our blessed Lord and Saviour.

| *Reflection by* **Malcolm Guite**

Psalms 54, **79** *or* 32, **36**
Jeremiah 18.1-12
John 10.1-10

# Tuesday 1 April

### John 10.1-10

*'I am the gate' (vv. 7, 9)*

We begin a chapter exploring what it means to call Jesus the Good Shepherd, a chapter that draws deeply on the daily experience of a pastoral people and also on the rich vein of pastoral imagery and metaphor in the Old Testament. But before we come to him as shepherd, Jesus offers an image of himself as a gate or door, in one of the seven key I AM sayings of this gospel: 'I AM the gate of the sheep.'

There is a local context for this saying: the sheep folds in the hill country were circular stone wall enclosures, with no door or roof, but a gap through which the sheep could pass into the safety of the enclosure and across which the shepherd would lie, making himself the door so that all who came or went must step across him. So, Jesus invites us to come in and go out through him. That phrase may itself be an echo of the promised blessing of Psalm 121.8, now fulfilled in Christ: 'The Lord will keep your going out and your coming in from this time on and for evermore.'

But there is something about Christ himself as a door that goes beyond this pastoral context. We come in prayer through Christ to the Father. In John 1.51 Christ becomes Jacob's ladder, becomes 'the very gate of heaven' or, in the words of John the Divine, 'a door open in heaven' (Revelation 4.1).

Merciful Lord,
you know our struggle to serve you:
when sin spoils our lives
and overshadows our hearts,
come to our aid
and turn us back to you again;
through Jesus Christ our Lord.

COLLECT

## Wednesday 2 April

Psalms 63, **90** *or* **34**
Jeremiah 18.13-end
John 10.11-21

### John 10.11-21

*'I am the Good Shepherd' (v.11)*

Now we come to the central I AM saying of this chapter: 'I AM the Good Shepherd.' The saying is so often given sentimental illustration that we miss the shock and scandal of it. By saying I AM (*ego eimi* in Greek) Jesus is identifying himself with Yahweh, the great I AM, and by saying that he is *the* Good Shepherd, he is claiming to be the same Lord and Shepherd who is proclaimed mysteriously in Psalm 23. I say mysteriously, because in verse 4 the psalmist claims that this Shepherd-Lord will lead us even through death itself: 'Even though I walk through the valley of the shadow of death... you are with me.'

The first hearers of this psalm must have been mystified. They knew that shepherds *lead* their sheep, pioneer the path for them, and that the sheep follow because they know the shepherd and trust that he has found a way through. How could Yawheh lead us through the gate of death? For he is immortal and cannot die! And then comes Jesus and says, 'I am He. I lay down my life for the sheep', and we note, with a sharp, tender shock, that the promise of Psalm 23 is preceded by the agony of Psalm 22, the crucifixion psalm. It is the agony of the one that makes the blessing of the other possible.

COLLECT

Merciful Lord,
absolve your people from their offences,
that through your bountiful goodness
we may all be delivered from the chains of those sins
which by our frailty we have committed;
grant this, heavenly Father,
for Jesus Christ's sake, our blessed Lord and Saviour.

| *Reflection by* **Malcolm Guite**

Psalms 53, **86** *or* **37***
Jeremiah 19.1-13
John 10.22-end

**Thursday 3 April**

### John 10.22-end

*'The Father and I are one' (v.30)*

John carefully locates this moment of revelation in time and place. It's set at the festival of the rededication of the Temple – Hannukah, the festival of lights – and is set in the Temple, specifically Solomon's Porch, which ran along one side of the court of the Gentiles. The one who said 'I am the Light of the world' now deepens his claim on a day that recalls the lights rekindled in the newly cleansed Temple when every other light had gone out.

The Temple was the meeting place of God and humanity, and now Jesus reveals that the true Temple, the true meeting place of God and humanity, comes to them as a person. The Temple has come to life and is now more than a mere meeting place, it is a place of union: 'the Father and I are One'. And this declaration does not take place, as one might have expected, in the sanctuary – the holy centre – but on the edge, the court of the Gentiles, the edge that is precisely the meeting place of Jew and Gentile. It is here that Jesus reveals, not only for one race or religion, but for all, that he and the Father are one.

'They tried to arrest him, but he escaped from their hands.' He escapes also from ours. We cannot confine the God-Human, the Human-God, to our categories, he breaks them all and walks free, beckoning us instead into his mystery.

Merciful Lord,
you know our struggle to serve you:
when sin spoils our lives
and overshadows our hearts,
come to our aid
and turn us back to you again;
through Jesus Christ our Lord.

COLLECT

# Friday 4 April

Psalm **102** *or* **31**
Jeremiah 19.14 – 20.6
John 11.1-16

## John 11.1-16

*'Let us also go, that we may die with him' (v.16)*

Thomas is a distinctive and attractive character among the twelve, and no more so than at this moment. He is often given to doubts, difficulties and gloomy prognostications – a natural pessimist. But at the same time he is strong-willed, intensely loyal and ready to do the right thing whatever the cost, which paradoxically makes the company's pet pessimist an encouraging person to be with! Others, swayed by naive optimism, begin an enterprise, and then when difficulties arise, give up. Thomas, by contrast, assumes that they are facing defeat but chooses to be with Jesus anyway and urges the others to do the same. One is reminded of Gimli's great one-liner in the film of the Lord of the Rings: 'Certainty of death. Small chance of success. What are we waiting for?' Or the words of the Earl when the English are losing the Battle of Maldon:

> 'Will shall be the sterner, heart the bolder,
> spirit the greater as our strength lessens.' (Tolkien's translation)

C. S. Lewis, too, created a character in his Narnia novels whose role is very like that of 'doubting Thomas': Puddleglum, the perpetually pessimistic Marsh Wiggle, who for all his gloomy prognostications, doubts and difficulties, is the one who hangs on to the quest and even says, 'I'm going to live like a Narnian even if there is no Narnia.'

Happily most churches have someone like this, someone who sees all the difficulties, but also stays to see them through.

COLLECT

Merciful Lord,
absolve your people from their offences,
that through your bountiful goodness
we may all be delivered from the chains of those sins
which by our frailty we have committed;
grant this, heavenly Father,
for Jesus Christ's sake, our blessed Lord and Saviour.

| *Reflection by* **Malcolm Guite**

# Saturday 5 April

### John 11.17-27

*'If you had been here ...' (v.21)*

John takes us from the most mind-expanding cosmic theology to the most intimate human experience, in almost the same breath, and no wonder, for John's contention is that because the Word was made flesh, great theology happens precisely in and through human intimacy, not least the intimacy of death and mourning.

Here Martha confronts Jesus with one of those agonizing 'if onlys' that haunt and torment the bereaved: 'If only I'd known..., if only he hadn't taken that route..., if only I could have been there...' And now the sharpest of these that almost blames the very person who has come to share your grief: 'If you had been here, my brother would not have died.' Jesus will soon be pierced by nails and a spear, but this too is heart-piercing, and he will hear it a second time from Martha's sister, Mary. He takes it, he absorbs it, but he is not thwarted by its implicit anger and accusation; he still has words of hope and comfort to bring.

If you visit the bereaved on behalf of the Church, you stand where Jesus stands here, amid the anger and the accusation, so often directed, as it must be, at God: 'If only he had intervened as surely he could – but no – he let us all down.' The only way to hear these things is to hear them in and with Jesus, and to meet them with his compassionate love.

Merciful Lord,
you know our struggle to serve you:
when sin spoils our lives
and overshadows our hearts,
come to our aid
and turn us back to you again;
through Jesus Christ our Lord.

COLLECT

*Reflection by* **Malcolm Guite** | 35

## Monday 7 April

Psalms **73**, 121 *or* **44**
Jeremiah 21.1-10
John 11.28-44

### John 11.28-44

*'... he cried with a loud voice' (v.43)*

'He speaks – and listening to his voice
New life the dead receive.'

In these lines from his famous hymn 'And can it be', Charles Wesley was alluding obliquely to the raising of Lazarus. The prologue to John's Gospel is in one sense the prologue and underpinning of every single episode in the whole book. John wants us to know that the one who 'cried out with a loud voice' is the Word himself, the one who spoke the cosmos into being. He is the Lord whose voice is celebrated in Psalm 29: 'The voice of the Lord is over the waters...The voice of the Lord is powerful; the voice of the Lord is full of majesty.' And now this primal creative voice speaks from within its own creation and raises the dead. And yet in this very passage, only a few verses earlier, this same all-powerful voice is weeping, sharing our tears, experiencing with us our misery and grief.

This gets to the heart of the matter. The Word really was made flesh. He is fully human and feels from within all the pain and devastation of our griefs, the 'thousand natural shocks that flesh is heir to' (*Hamlet*, Act 3, Scene 1). And that is why, even in this life, he can raise us too from the dead. He has been in the places where we are dead or dying: the heartbreak, the fear, the failure. Even as he weeps with us, his creating voice raises and releases us.

COLLECT

Most merciful God,
who by the death and resurrection of your Son Jesus Christ
delivered and saved the world:
grant that by faith in him who suffered on the cross
we may triumph in the power of his victory;
through Jesus Christ our Lord.

*Reflection by* **Malcolm Guite**

Psalms **35**, 123 *or* **48**, 52
Jeremiah 22.1-5, 13-19
John 11.45-end

# Tuesday 8 April

### John 11.45-end

*'... better for ... one man to die' (v.50)*

It is remarkable that whatever is said of Jesus in the Gospel, even misunderstandings or downright attacks, he takes and transforms into blessings, not on himself, but on us. They call him 'the friend of sinners' to denigrate him, and he is forever, and to our immense blessing, the friend of sinners, for he came to befriend us. Mary Magdalene 'mistook' him for a gardener, but he was in truth The Gardener, who had planted the garden of the world, who had turned the garden of mourning into the garden of resurrection, and he is a gardener to Mary's heart, wintry with grief, for, as Lancelot Andrewes said, 'with one word he makes all green again'.

So here Caiaphas, thinking that he speaks of nothing more than political expediency, suggests that Jesus should be sacrificed to save the nation, a sordid attempt to make the end justify the means, but Jesus fulfils his words in a far better way and far beyond his imaginings, for he dies to save not just one nation but the whole world, indeed the cosmos (*ton kosmon* is how John puts 'world' in 3.16).

From here on Jesus is a wanted man, in many senses. Those who gather for the Passover are looking for him with hope as a Messiah, those who want to preserve the status quo are looking for him to destroy him. The great question is 'Will he come?'

Gracious Father,
you gave up your Son
out of love for the world:
lead us to ponder the mysteries of his passion,
that we may know eternal peace
through the shedding of our Saviour's blood,
Jesus Christ our Lord.

COLLECT

*Reflection by* **Malcolm Guite** | 37

## **Wednesday 9 April**

Psalms **55**, 124 *or* **119.57-80**
Jeremiah 22.20 – 23.8
John 12.1-11

### John 12.1-11

*'The house was filled with the fragrance' (v.3)*

After so much public drama and political tension, and before the violent climax of his story, John gives us by contrast this poignant, intimate interlude: the anointing at Bethany. As so often in the gospels, the behaviour of the men contrasts unfavourably with that of the women. Many commentators rightly contrast Judas and Mary. Judas sees only the price of the perfume, whereas Mary, with her extravagant gesture, recognizes the infinite value of her saviour's love. Here Judas illustrates perfectly Oscar Wilde's quip that a cynic is one 'who knows the price of everything and the value of nothing'. The real poetry of this moment, though, is the way Mary's love anticipates Christ's death yet somehow gestures beyond it, something I tried to intimate in a poem of my own:

> Come close with Mary, Martha, Lazarus,
> So close the candles flare with their soft breath,
> And kindle heart and soul to flame within us
> Lit by these mysteries of life and death.
> For beauty now begins the final movement,
> In quietness and intimate encounter,
> The alabaster jar of precious ointment
> Is broken open for the world's true lover.
> The whole room richly fills to feast the senses
> With all the yearning such a fragrance brings,
> The heart is mourning but the spirit dances,
> Here at the very centre of all things,
> Here at the meeting place of love and loss
> We all foresee and see beyond the cross.

(From *Sounding the Seasons*)

**COLLECT**

Most merciful God,
who by the death and resurrection of your Son Jesus Christ
delivered and saved the world:
grant that by faith in him who suffered on the cross
we may triumph in the power of his victory;
through Jesus Christ our Lord.

*Reflection by* **Malcolm Guite**

Psalms **40**, 125 *or* 56, **57** (63\*)       **Thursday 10 April**
Jeremiah 23.9-32
John 12.12-19

### John 12.12-19

*'... the world has gone after him' (v.19)*

Once again something is said of Jesus that is far truer than those who utter it could have imagined. The crowds that surged towards Jesus on Palm Sunday were devout Jews, there in Jerusalem for the Passover, the very ceremony that distinguished Jews from the rest of the world and defined them as a nation: a chosen and exceptional people.

The psalm they quoted in their Hosannas, Psalm 118, was a distinctly messianic and royal psalm. The prophecy they saw fulfilled in Jesus' riding on a donkey was a distinctive prophecy to them alone. Both those who welcome Jesus and those who oppose him at this moment are Jewish people, taking a position about whether or not he is the longed-for Messiah. Perhaps the Pharisees only meant 'the whole world' as an exaggerated synonym for 'this big Passover crowd – our fellow Jews', but the word they use for 'the whole world' at this point is the very word Jesus uses earlier in John 3.16 for his universal mission 'God so loved the world (*'ho kosmos'*) that he sent his only Son.'

This deeper, more inclusive meaning of the word, this evocation of a mission of love to the Gentiles, is about to have its beginning in the very next verse of this Gospel when 'some Greeks' ask to see Jesus.

COLLECT

Gracious Father,
you gave up your Son
out of love for the world:
lead us to ponder the mysteries of his passion,
that we may know eternal peace
through the shedding of our Saviour's blood,
Jesus Christ our Lord.

# Friday 11 April

Psalms **22**, 126 *or* **51**, 54
Jeremiah 24
John 12.20-36*a*

### John 12.20-36*a*

*'The hour has come ...' (v.23)*

Back in chapter 2 of his Gospel, John set up a kind of tension and suspense in his narrative when Jesus says to his mother at the wedding at Cana, 'My hour has not yet come.' Thereafter we are always asking ourselves, 'When will it come? When is the moment we are waiting for?' Not just a sign, like the miracle at Cana, but the full revelation of who Jesus is.

Now, ten chapters later, that tension is released, that promise is fulfilled, and he announces at last, 'The hour has come!' And the fulfilment is initiated, not by some grand miracle or fulfilment of ancient prophecy, but with the arrival of 'some Greeks', a group of complete strangers who, according to the Jewish view, are not even supposed to be part of this story. This is so shocking and unexpected that Philip, whom the Greeks probably approached because he had a Greek name, goes off to consult Andrew, and then the two of them, stymied by this development, go to see Jesus, which is what Philip should have done in the first place.

It wouldn't be the only time that the question of 'who belongs?', 'who can come to Jesus?' was met by the Church with embarrassment and prevarication; we are in the middle of such a moment now with issues of sexuality and gender identity, but there is no doubt of Jesus' response: 'Welcome them, my death and my resurrection are for the whole world.'

COLLECT

Most merciful God,
who by the death and resurrection of your Son Jesus Christ
delivered and saved the world:
grant that by faith in him who suffered on the cross
we may triumph in the power of his victory;
through Jesus Christ our Lord.

*Reflection by* **Malcolm Guite**

# Saturday 12 April

### John 12.36*b*-end

*'I have come as light into the world' (v.46)*

Once more we hear that glorious, all-inclusive little phrase 'the world' – *ton kosmon* – ringing out from Jesus' lips, as John deftly returns us to the great theme of light shining in darkness, a theme he had announced in his prologue and developed so powerfully in chapters 8 and 9. We are not merely to long for light, or to 'believe in the light', or even to 'have the light'; we are, in a breathtaking command and promise, to 'become children of light'! For that is our truest life.

Did we not hear in the prologue, 'In him was life and the life was the light of all people' (John 1.4)? And now, in the presence of the Gentiles, and, with them, the whole world for which he dies, Jesus explicitly proclaims: 'I have come as the light of the world.' This is a light that does more than simply illuminate, it calls us into personal communion, something I tried to express in my sonnet on Christ as light:

> [Light] shimmers through translucent leaves in summer,
> Or spills from silver veins in leaden skies,
> It gathers in the candles at our vespers
> It concentrates in tiny drops of dew,
> At times it sings for joy, at times it whispers,
> But all the time it calls me back to you.
> I follow you upstream through this dark night
> My saviour, source, and spring, my life and light.

(from *Parable and Paradox*)

Gracious Father,
you gave up your Son
out of love for the world:
lead us to ponder the mysteries of his passion,
that we may know eternal peace
through the shedding of our Saviour's blood,
Jesus Christ our Lord.

COLLECT

*Reflection by* **Malcolm Guite**    41

## **Monday 14 April**
Monday of Holy Week

Psalm 41
Lamentations 1.1-12*a*
Luke 22.1-23

### Lamentations 1.1-12*a*

*'... all her friends have dealt treacherously with her' (v.2)*

Lamentations graphically describes the devastation of Jerusalem and the appalling suffering of her people: brutal slaughter, people enslaved or turned into refugees, children starving, women raped, the destruction not only of homes and public and religious buildings but also of a culture, a political community, and a whole way of life, and betrayal by 'all her friends'. In the face of all this, the overwhelming response is lament. This is as relevant to our world as it was then. If our prayer does not include lament, we are not seeing the world as it is – or the Church as it is, or ourselves as we are. It is right to lament, grieve, cry out, weep, mourn, be in anguish.

Holy Week is a time for lament, for realistically facing up to what and who have gone terribly wrong. This is a way of realizing the scale of our salvation, and what it was that faced Jesus, 'the Lamb of God who takes away the sin of the world' (John 1.29). This unique person, who is utterly at one with God and with us, engages with the depths of suffering, sin and death. A key element in this is that one of his close friends, Judas, betrayed him.

Why is breaking trust so fundamental? I think it is because what Jesus most desires is mutual love – between himself and us, and among ourselves. But without mutual trust that is impossible.

COLLECT | Almighty and everlasting God,
who in your tender love towards the human race
    sent your Son our Saviour Jesus Christ
to take upon him our flesh
and to suffer death upon the cross:
grant that we may follow the example of his patience and humility,
and also be made partakers of his resurrection;
through Jesus Christ our Lord.

42 | *Reflection by* **David Ford**

Psalm 27
Lamentations 3.1-18
Luke 22. [24-38] 39-53

## Tuesday 15 April
Tuesday of Holy Week

### Luke 22. [24-38] 39-53

*'Father, ... not my will but yours be done' (v.42)*

The Greek word *thelēma* means 'desire' as well as 'will', as here and in the Lord's Prayer. In Israel's scriptures, and in the teaching of Jesus, at the heart of God's will and desire for us is that we find our fulfilment in loving God with all our heart, mind and strength, and loving our neighbours as ourselves.

Jesus embodies such love, and twice in the Gospel of Luke we are given an insight into how he resists temptations to let other desires have priority. At the beginning of his ministry the temptations involve his desires for food, for worldly power and glory, and for doing spectacular, impressive signs (Luke 4.1-13). Here, at the climax of his life, the temptation is to turn away from the depths of suffering, sin and death in his crucifixion. His ultimate test is to be willing to go that way of love 'to the end' (John 13.1), in loving solidarity with all who suffer, sin and die, and to lay down his life in order to open up to others his own deep relationship of love with his Father and with all who trust him.

We live in cultures saturated with stimuli to desires of many sorts. To receive and trust Jesus is to begin to have our desires continually inspired and transformed by him. In this, the prayer of Jesus himself is crucial – and still continues (Hebrews 7.25).

True and humble king,
hailed by the crowd as Messiah:
grant us the faith to know you and love you,
that we may be found beside you
on the way of the cross,
which is the path of glory.

COLLECT

*Reflection by* **David Ford** | 43

## **Wednesday 16 April**

Wednesday of Holy Week

Psalm 102 [*or* 102.1-18]
Wisdom 1.16 – 2.1; 2.12-22
*or* Jeremiah 11.18-20
Luke 22.54-end

### Luke 22.54-end

*'I am not!' (v.58)*

What relationships are at the heart of our identity? With whom do we really belong?

As Jesus is put on trial, someone says to Peter, 'You also are one of them.' Peter's 'I am not!' is not only a lie, it denies his core identity, who he has become through Jesus calling him, giving him a new name and community. In the trial, Jesus' identity is central: Messiah (Christ)? Son of Man? Son of God? King of the Jews? In stark contrast to Peter, Jesus refuses to deny such dangerous religious and political identities and is condemned to be crucified.

Holy Week is a time to consider and renew our core identity. In many Christian communities today, as in the early Church, Easter is a time for baptisms and renewal of the promises made in baptism. Baptism is about our fundamental identity, centred on being baptized into the death and resurrection of Jesus, and belonging utterly to God and to each other 'in Christ'.

Other forms of belonging (family, gender, race, class, nation, job, politics, culture, friendships, networks, online groups, etc.) may harmonize with this or be in tension with it. In our situation of identities in conflict, we need continual wise discernment, and freedom from fear, in order to decide, given the utter primacy of our baptism, on the extent and quality of our commitment to other identities and relationships.

C O L L E C T | Almighty and everlasting God,
who in your tender love towards the human race
    sent your Son our Saviour Jesus Christ
to take upon him our flesh
and to suffer death upon the cross:
grant that we may follow the example of his patience and humility,
and also be made partakers of his resurrection;
through Jesus Christ our Lord.

| *Reflection by* **David Ford**

Psalms 42, 43
Leviticus 16.2-24
Luke 23.1-25

## Thursday 17 April
Maundy Thursday

### Luke 23.1-25

*'Pilate asked him, "Are you the king of the Jews?"' (v.3)*

In Luke's account, the accusations against Jesus when he is brought before the Roman governor are angled towards Pilate's interests in public order, taxes for the Emperor and claims to be a king. In the Roman Empire the only people who could be kings were those appointed by the Emperor, and any others were treated as rebels.

The reply of Jesus to Pilate's question is, 'You say so.' We can understand why this is not a 'yes' or 'no' response.

From the beginning of Luke's Gospel, Jesus is associated with 'the throne of his ancestor David ... and of his kingdom there will be no end' (1.32-33). But, as the Gospel unfolds, there are many surprises about the sort of king he is. He resists the tempting offer of power over all the kingdoms of the world. He inaugurates the 'kingdom of God' with healings, exorcisms, forgiveness, good news for the poor, uncomfortable news for the rich and teaching about the shockingly generous love of God for us, and about our love for our neighbours. Little children and daring friendships with prostitutes and hated tax collectors are central to this kingdom.

But, above all, this kingdom is inseparable from who Jesus is and what happens to him. Maundy Thursday reveals his upside-down power of loving, humble service: 'I am among you as one who serves.' How could Pilate have begun to understand this sort of king? How can we?

True and humble king,
hailed by the crowd as Messiah:
grant us the faith to know you and love you,
that we may be found beside you
on the way of the cross,
which is the path of glory.

COLLECT

# Friday 18 April
Good Friday

Psalm 69
Genesis 22.1-18
Hebrews 10.1-10

### Genesis 22.1-18

*'Here I am!' (vv.1, 7, 11)*

'Here I am!' Abraham says this three times – to God, who calls him by name, 'Abraham!'; to his only, beloved son, Isaac, calling him, 'Father!'; and to 'the angel of the Lord' calling him, 'Abraham! Abraham!' In this test, who Abraham is in his deepest relationships, his 'I am', is at stake. Is utter trust in God at the heart of his identity? Is God utterly trustworthy? Can God be trusted with our most precious and intimate relationships? Is breaking trust with God something worse even than the death of those we love – who are ultimately all in God's hands?

'Here I am!' On Good Friday, Jesus, the beloved Son of God, who has said to his Father, 'See, I have come to do your will' or 'your desire', gives himself utterly in love for his Father and for us. It is the deepest mystery, this 'once for all' event. It is central to the 'I am' of Jesus, to the 'I am' of God, and to the love in which we are invited to trust, as Abraham trusted.

'Here I am!' As we stand at the foot of the cross, how do we receive the One who calls each of us by name, and gives himself for us and to us?

COLLECT

Almighty Father,
look with mercy on this your family
for which our Lord Jesus Christ was content to be betrayed
    and given up into the hands of sinners
    and to suffer death upon the cross;
who is alive and glorified with you and the Holy Spirit,
one God, now and for ever.

| *Reflection by* **David Ford**

Psalm 142
Hosea 6.1-6
John 2.18-22

**Saturday 19 April**
Easter Eve

### John 2.18-22

*'What sign can you show us ... ?' (v.18)*

Jesus identifies the Temple, which he has earlier called 'my Father's house' (his family home), with his body, which will be destroyed, and then 'in three days I will raise it up'. This is the greatest of all the signs in John's Gospel, the death and resurrection of Jesus, which creates the new family home. This home is nothing less than himself and his love: 'Abide in me as I abide in you ... As the Father has loved me, so I have loved you: abide in my love' (John 15.4, 9). Approaching death he prays, 'As you, Father, are in me and I am in you, may they also be in us, so that the world may believe that you have sent me ...' (John 17.21). What a home!

But good homes can cost a lot. Today, on Holy Saturday, we sit with the dark mystery of death itself. What was happening when Jesus was dead? Death had happened to him, along with suffering, sin and evil. *But he had also happened to death, suffering, sin and evil.* This unique person – utterly human and mortal, yet also utterly divine – dies and also transforms death itself, along with suffering, sin and evil. 'In three days I will raise it up.' The ultimate sign that death, and the darkness of suffering, sin and evil, do not in reality have the last word, is that Good Friday and Holy Saturday lead into Easter Day.

Grant, Lord,
that we who are baptized into the death
of your Son our Saviour Jesus Christ
may continually put to death our evil desires
and be buried with him;
and that through the grave and gate of death
we may pass to our joyful resurrection;
through his merits,
who died and was buried and rose again for us,
your Son Jesus Christ our Lord.

COLLECT

*Reflection by* **David Ford**    47

## Morning Prayer – a simple form

*Preparation*

O Lord, open our lips
**and our mouth shall proclaim your praise.**

A prayer of thanksgiving for Lent *(for Passiontide see p. 50)*

Blessed are you, Lord God of our salvation,
to you be glory and praise for ever.
In the darkness of our sin you have shone in our hearts
to give the light of the knowledge of the glory of God
in the face of Jesus Christ.
Open our eyes to acknowledge your presence,
that freed from the misery of sin and shame
we may grow into your likeness from glory to glory.
Blessed be God, Father, Son and Holy Spirit.
**Blessed be God for ever.**

*Word of God*

Psalmody *(the psalm or psalms listed for the day)*

**Glory to the Father and to the Son
and to the Holy Spirit;
as it was in the beginning is now:
and shall be for ever. Amen.**

Reading from Holy Scripture *(one or both of the passages set for the day)*

Reflection

The Benedictus (The Song of Zechariah) *(see opposite page)*

*Prayers*

Intercessions – a time of prayer for the day and its tasks, the world and its need, the church and her life.

The Collect for the Day

The Lord's Prayer *(see p. 51)*

*Conclusion*

A blessing or the Grace *(see p. 51)*, or a concluding response

Let us bless the Lord
**Thanks be to God**

## Benedictus (The Song of Zechariah)

1 Blessed be the Lord the God of Israel, ♦
who has come to his people and set them free.

2 He has raised up for us a mighty Saviour, ♦
born of the house of his servant David.

3 Through his holy prophets God promised of old ♦
to save us from our enemies,
from the hands of all that hate us,

4 To show mercy to our ancestors, ♦
and to remember his holy covenant.

5 This was the oath God swore to our father Abraham: ♦
to set us free from the hands of our enemies,

6 Free to worship him without fear, ♦
holy and righteous in his sight
all the days of our life.

7 And you, child, shall be called the prophet of the Most High, ♦
for you will go before the Lord to prepare his way,

8 To give his people knowledge of salvation ♦
by the forgiveness of all their sins.

9 In the tender compassion of our God ♦
the dawn from on high shall break upon us,

10 To shine on those who dwell in darkness
and the shadow of death, ♦
and to guide our feet into the way of peace.

*Luke 1.68-79*

**Glory to the Father and to the Son
and to the Holy Spirit;
as it was in the beginning is now:
and shall be for ever. Amen.**

## Seasonal Prayers of Thanksgiving

---

*Passiontide*

Blessed are you, Lord God of our salvation,
to you be praise and glory for ever.
As a man of sorrows and acquainted with grief
your only Son was lifted up
that he might draw the whole world to himself.
May we walk this day in the way of the cross
and always be ready to share its weight,
declaring your love for all the world.
Blessed be God, Father, Son and Holy Spirit.
**Blessed be God for ever.**

---

*At Any Time*

Blessed are you, creator of all,
to you be praise and glory for ever.
As your dawn renews the face of the earth
bringing light and life to all creation,
may we rejoice in this day you have made;
as we wake refreshed from the depths of sleep,
open our eyes to behold your presence
and strengthen our hands to do your will,
that the world may rejoice and give you praise.
Blessed be God, Father, Son and Holy Spirit.
**Blessed be God for ever.**

*after Lancelot Andrewes (1626)*

## The Lord's Prayer and The Grace

Our Father in heaven,
hallowed be your name,
your kingdom come,
your will be done,
on earth as in heaven.
Give us today our daily bread.
Forgive us our sins
as we forgive those who sin against us.
Lead us not into temptation
but deliver us from evil.
For the kingdom, the power,
and the glory are yours
now and for ever.
Amen.

*(or)*

Our Father, who art in heaven,
hallowed be thy name;
thy kingdom come;
thy will be done;
on earth as it is in heaven.
Give us this day our daily bread.
And forgive us our trespasses,
as we forgive those who trespass against us.
And lead us not into temptation;
but deliver us from evil.
For thine is the kingdom,
the power and the glory,
for ever and ever.
Amen.

The grace of our Lord Jesus Christ,
and the love of God,
and the fellowship of the Holy Spirit,
be with us all evermore.
Amen.

# An Order for Night Prayer (Compline)

## Preparation

The Lord almighty grant us a quiet night and a perfect end.
**Amen.**

Our help is in the name of the Lord
**who made heaven and earth.**

*A period of silence for reflection on the past day may follow.*

*The following or other suitable words of penitence may be used*

**Most merciful God,
we confess to you,
before the whole company of heaven and one another,
that we have sinned in thought, word and deed
and in what we have failed to do.
Forgive us our sins,
heal us by your Spirit
and raise us to new life in Christ. Amen.**

O God, make speed to save us.
**O Lord, make haste to help us.**

**Glory to the Father and to the Son
and to the Holy Spirit;
as it was in the beginning is now
and shall be for ever. Amen.
Alleluia.**

*The following or another suitable hymn may be sung*

Before the ending of the day,
Creator of the world, we pray
That you, with steadfast love, would keep
Your watch around us while we sleep.

From evil dreams defend our sight,
From fears and terrors of the night;
Tread underfoot our deadly foe
That we no sinful thought may know.

O Father, that we ask be done
Through Jesus Christ, your only Son;
And Holy Spirit, by whose breath
Our souls are raised to life from death.

# The Word of God

*Psalmody*

*One or more of Psalms 4, 91 or 134 may be used.*

*Psalm 134*

1  Come, bless the Lord, all you servants of the Lord, ♦
   you that by night stand in the house of the Lord.

2  Lift up your hands towards the sanctuary ♦
   and bless the Lord.

3  The Lord who made heaven and earth ♦
   give you blessing out of Zion.

**Glory to the Father and to the Son
and to the Holy Spirit;
as it was in the beginning is now
and shall be for ever. Amen.**

*Scripture Reading*

*One of the following short lessons or another suitable
passage is read*

You, O Lord, are in the midst of us and we are called by your
name; leave us not, O Lord our God.

*Jeremiah 14.9*

*(or)*

Be sober, be vigilant, because your adversary the devil is
prowling round like a roaring lion, seeking for someone
to devour. Resist him, strong in the faith.

*I Peter 5.8,9*

*(or)*

The servants of the Lamb shall see the face of God, whose name
will be on their foreheads. There will be no more night: they will
not need the light of a lamp or the light of the sun, for God will
be their light, and they will reign for ever and ever.

*Revelation 22.4,5*

*The following responsory may be said*

Into your hands, O Lord, I commend my spirit.
**Into your hands, O Lord, I commend my spirit.**
For you have redeemed me, Lord God of truth.
**I commend my spirit.**
Glory to the Father and to the Son
and to the Holy Spirit.
**Into your hands, O Lord, I commend my spirit.**

*Or, in Easter*

Into your hands, O Lord, I commend my spirit.
    Alleluia, alleluia.
**Into your hands, O Lord, I commend my spirit.**
    **Alleluia, alleluia.**
For you have redeemed me, Lord God of truth.
**Alleluia, alleluia.**
Glory to the Father and to the Son
and to the Holy Spirit.
**Into your hands, O Lord, I commend my spirit.**
    **Alleluia, alleluia.**

Keep me as the apple of your eye.
**Hide me under the shadow of your wings.**

*Gospel Canticle*

*Nunc Dimittis (The Song of Simeon)*

**Save us, O Lord, while waking,**
**and guard us while sleeping,**
**that awake we may watch with Christ**
**and asleep may rest in peace.**

1    Now, Lord, you let your servant go in peace:
     your word has been fulfilled.

2    My own eyes have seen the salvation
     which you have prepared in the sight of every people;

3    A light to reveal you to the nations
     and the glory of your people Israel.

*Luke 2.29-32*

Glory to the Father and to the Son
and to the Holy Spirit;
as it was in the beginning is now
and shall be for ever. Amen.

Save us, O Lord, while waking,
and guard us while sleeping,
that awake we may watch with Christ
and asleep may rest in peace.

## Prayers

*Intercessions and thanksgivings may be offered here.*

### The Collect

Visit this place, O Lord, we pray,
and drive far from it the snares of the enemy;
may your holy angels dwell with us and guard us in peace,
and may your blessing be always upon us;
through Jesus Christ our Lord.
**Amen.**

*The Lord's Prayer (see p. 51) may be said.*

## The Conclusion

In peace we will lie down and sleep;
**for you alone, Lord, make us dwell in safety.**

Abide with us, Lord Jesus,
**for the night is at hand and the day is now past.**

As the night watch looks for the morning,
**so do we look for you, O Christ.**

[Come with the dawning of the day
**and make yourself known in the breaking of the bread.]**

The Lord bless us and watch over us;
the Lord make his face shine upon us and be gracious to us;
the Lord look kindly on us and give us peace.
**Amen.**

# Love what you've read?

Why not consider using
*Reflections for Daily Prayer*
all year round? We also
publish these meditations on
Bible readings in an annual
format, containing material
for the entire Church year.

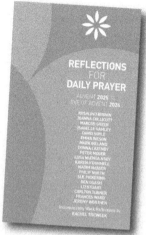

The volume for 2025/26 will
be published in May 2025
and features contributions
from a host of distinguished
writers including: **Rosalind
Brown, Joanna Collicutt,
Marcus Green, Isabelle
Hamley, David Hoyle, Emma
Ineson, Mark Ireland, Donna Lazenby, Peter Moger,
Lusa Nsenga Ngoy, Karen O'Donnell, Nadim Nasser,
Philip North, Sue Pickering, Ben Quash, Liz Stuart,
Carlton Turner, Frances Ward** and **Jeremy Worthen**.

The reflections for Holy Week 2026 are written by
**Rachel Treweek**.

**Reflections for Daily Prayer:
Advent 2025 to the eve of Advent 2026**

ISBN 978 1 78140 497 3
334 pages • Available May 2025

## Can't wait for next year?

You can still pick up this year's edition of *Reflections*,
direct from us (at **www.chpublishing.co.uk**) or from
your local Christian bookshop.

**Reflections for Daily Prayer:
Advent 2024 to the eve of Advent 2025**

ISBN 978 1 78140 457 7
334 pages • Available now

# REFLECTIONS FOR DAILY PRAYER
## App

Make Bible study and reflection a part of your routine wherever you go with the Reflections for Daily Prayer App for Apple and Android devices.

Download the app for free from the App Store (Apple devices) or Google Play (Android devices) and receive a week's worth of reflections free. Then purchase a monthly, three-monthly or annual subscription to receive up-to-date content.

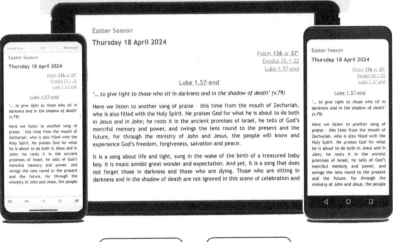

# REFLECTIONS FOR SUNDAYS (YEAR C)

*Reflections for Sundays* offers over 250 reflections on the Principal Readings for every Sunday and major Holy Day in Year C, from the same experienced team of writers that have made *Reflections for Daily Prayer* so successful. For each Sunday and major Holy Day, they provide:

- full lectionary details for the Principal Service
- a reflection on each Old Testament reading (both Continuous and Related)
- a reflection on the Epistle
- a reflection on the Gospel.

This book also contains a substantial introduction to the Gospel of Luke, written by **Paula Gooder.**

**288 pages**
**ISBN 978 1 78140 039 5**

> **Also available in Kindle and epub formats**

# REFLECTIONS ON THE PSALMS

**192 pages**
**ISBN 978 0 7151 4490 9**

*Reflections on the Psalms* provides original and insightful meditations on each of the Bible's 150 Psalms.

Each reflection is accompanied by its corresponding Psalm refrain and prayer from the *Common Worship Psalter*, making this a valuable resource for personal or devotional use.

Specially written introductions by **Paula Gooder** and **Steven Croft** explore the Psalms and the Bible and the Psalms in the life of the Church.